HAMMER & SAW

An Introduction to Woodworking

Also by Harvey Weiss

Harvey Weiss

HAMMER & SAW

An Introduction to Woodworking

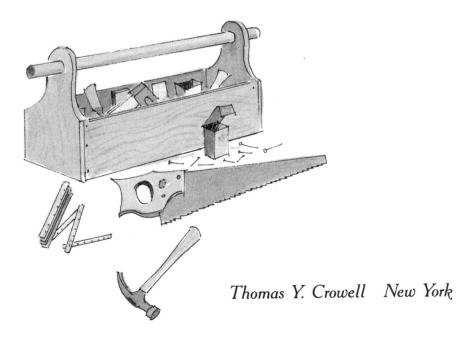

Thomas Y. Crowell   New York

Library of Congress Cataloging in Publication Data
Weiss, Harvey.
    Hammer and saw.

    SUMMARY: Includes basic instructions on how to choose,
measure, and saw wood, hammer in nails, drill holes, and
finish wood surfaces.
    1. Woodwork—Juvenile literature.   [1. Woodwork]
I. Title.
TT185.W42 1981   684′.08   81-43032
ISBN 0-690-04130-6   AACR2
ISBN 0-690-04131-4 (lib. bdg.)

 4   5   6   7   8   9   10

Contents

Introduction

Wood is a basic material in our lives. It is everywhere around us. Houses are built of it. Most of the furniture we use is made of it. In fact, the very paper this book is printed on is probably made from wood pulp. The pencil I have by my side is a piece of graphite surrounded by wood—and there is a great big tree outside my window that is growing a little larger every year and that could be cut down (though I certainly hope it won't be) and sawed into a great many sturdy, usable planks.

Wood is one of the most widely available materials, is fairly inexpensive, and comes in many sizes and shapes.

The first part of this book is about how to use wood. It will tell you just what is involved in cutting, shaping, and assembling wood—what tools are needed and how to use them. The second part of the book describes a variety of simple projects that can be built by even the most inexperienced woodworker.

Most of us take for granted the simple sawing of a board or the banging in of a nail. But there is a right way and a wrong way of doing anything. The right way is the best and the easiest way, and this book tries to show it to you.

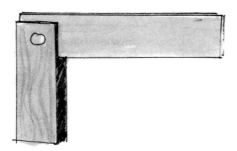

This is a try square. The wood part and the steel blade are at exact right angles to each other. The try square can be used as a straight edge or to check if a board is warped, or to see if two boards are at right angles to each other.

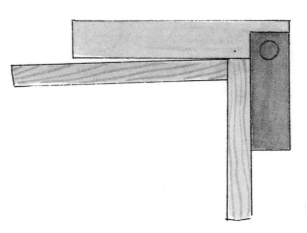

In this example the try square tells us that the two boards being checked have not been nailed together exactly at right angles. (If they were at right angles there would be no gap between the blade of the try square and the horizontal board.)

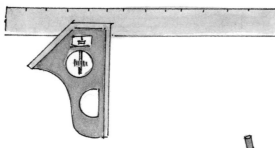

This is called a combination square. It is all metal. The blade can be shifted by means of an adjustment screw. The tool can be used as a try square as well as for a variety of measuring tasks.

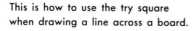
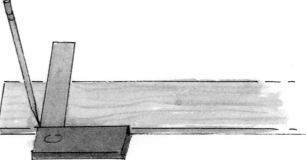

This is how to use the try square when drawing a line across a board.

1. How to Saw Wood

Suppose you have a board and want to cut a piece off the end of it. How should you go about it?

You will, of course, need a saw. The type you are most likely to have in your house is a common 24-tooth cross-cut saw like the one shown in the illustration.

You will also need a pencil line on the board that tells you where to cut. You won't get an accurate cut if you trust your eye or simply guess at where to cut. In order to get a line squarely across a board, you need something called a try square. If the bottom, or thick edge, of the try square is held snugly up against the board, as shown in the illustration, the thin ruler edge will lie at an exact right angle across the board. The pencil line is drawn along the ruler edge.

Before you start to cut the board there is one more thing to consider. How are you going to support the wood

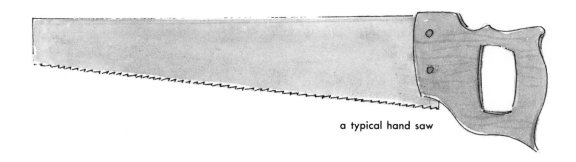

a typical hand saw

as you saw it? If you balance it on a pile of books or a wobbly little stool or a collapsing cardboard carton, you won't get a neat cut. The wood should be firmly supported.

If you are lucky enough to have a workbench with a vise, everything will go easily. Otherwise you will have to find a sturdy box or an old chair or some other solid surface on which to place the wood.

Large pieces of wood that won't fit into a vise, or that are too large to hold with a "C" clamp, can be rested on a wood box or similar support.

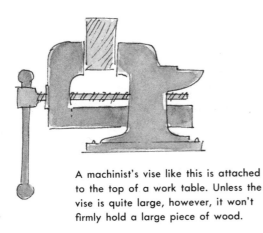

A machinist's vise like this is attached to the top of a work table. Unless the vise is quite large, however, it won't firmly hold a large piece of wood.

A woodworking vise is attached to the edge of the work bench. The jaws are wood so that the work is not marred when the vise is tightened.

One good way to hold down a piece of wood you are working on is with a metal "C" clamp like this. "C" clamps come in many different sizes.

scrap piece of wood to protect work

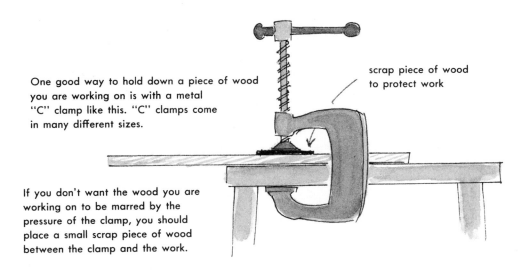

If you don't want the wood you are working on to be marred by the pressure of the clamp, you should place a small scrap piece of wood between the clamp and the work.

This is another kind of clamp that woodworkers often use.

A heavyweight assistant will help steady a long board while you are cutting it.

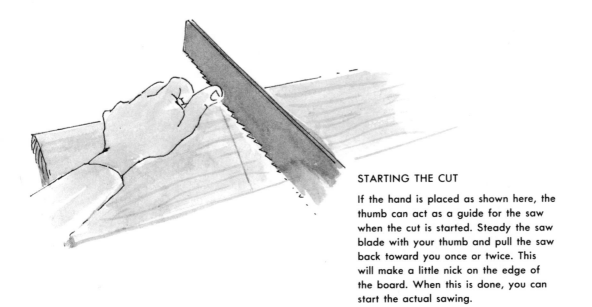

If the hand is placed as shown here, the thumb can act as a guide for the saw when the cut is started. Steady the saw blade with your thumb and pull the saw back toward you once or twice. This will make a little nick on the edge of the board. When this is done, you can start the actual sawing.

Doing the Cutting

If the saw is sharp and the wood held securely in place, the actual cutting is simple and won't require strenuous effort. You shouldn't have to use any heavy pressure on the saw. Just push it back and forth, letting the saw do the work. The actual cutting is done on the forward, or pushing, stroke.

If your arm gets tired, take a rest. Don't try to speed up the job by using two hands on the saw. If you get impatient and rush to finish the cut, the saw blade is liable to go off at an angle or stray from your guideline.

When the cut is almost completed, use one hand to support the piece of wood that is being removed. Unless you hold it up, the piece will fall away just before you complete the cut, probably tearing off a large splinter of wood.

About Saws

The trouble with saws that have been banging around the house for years is that they are usually dull. A dull saw is difficult to work with and won't do a good job. If it seems to take a great deal of effort to make a cut with your saw, the chances are that it is due for a sharpening. You may be able to find a place that specializes in sharpening tools. Or you can take the saw to a hardware store. Most good hardware stores have a saw-sharpening service. You may have to leave the saw there, but when you pick it up a week or so later, it will be as good as new.

Like all tools, saws come in a great variety of sizes and shapes.

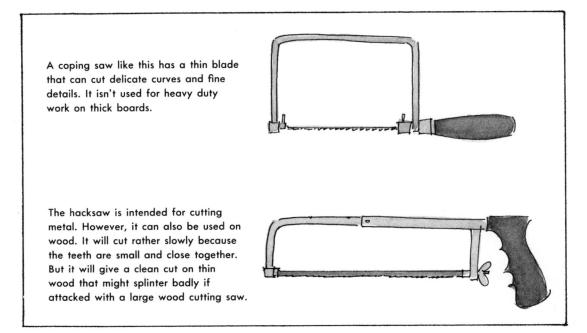

A coping saw like this has a thin blade that can cut delicate curves and fine details. It isn't used for heavy duty work on thick boards.

The hacksaw is intended for cutting metal. However, it can also be used on wood. It will cut rather slowly because the teeth are small and close together. But it will give a clean cut on thin wood that might splinter badly if attacked with a large wood cutting saw.

The backsaw has a metal strip along the top of the blade that keeps the saw rigid. It produces a neat, smooth cut and is a saw much used by skilled cabinet makers.

The keyhole saw, sometimes called a compass saw, can also cut curves. It has a very narrow blade that can be inserted in a hole bored in the wood.

Both the crosscut saw and the ripsaw are shaped like this.

The kind of saw that is most often used is called a crosscut saw. It is used to cut across the grain of the wood. (Pages 27–29 explain wood grain.) When you want to cut along or with the grain of the wood, you would ordinarily use a ripsaw. This saw has teeth that are designed to cut best in this situation. It looks very much like a crosscut saw. The easiest way to tell the difference between the saws is to look closely at the teeth. A ripsaw has teeth that are sharpened straight across. A crosscut saw has teeth that are sharpened at an angle.

You can tell the difference between a crosscut saw and a ripsaw by looking very closely at the teeth.

If the edges of the teeth look like this, you have a ripsaw.

straight across

If the edges of the teeth look like this, you have a crosscut saw.

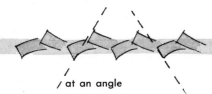

at an angle

14

Professional woodworkers and carpenters use many different types of power saws. But these can be dangerous unless they are properly handled. If you have access to tools of this sort, be sure you have been carefully and thoroughly instructed in their use before touching them.

Lumbermen use gasoline-powered chain saws nowadays to cut up large trees. But years ago long saws and strong men did the work.

2. How to Nail

Banging a nail into a piece of wood may seem like a pretty simple thing to do. And, generally speaking, it is. However, there are some things to watch out for. Choosing the right nail is the most important consideration. Too big a nail will split a piece of wood. Too small a nail won't hold two pieces of wood together.

A hammer, like a nail, is something we take for granted. But there are all kinds of hammers. The other day I took a count of the hammers that I have in my shop and was somewhat amazed to find that I actually own fifteen of them. That includes a few duplicates and a few that I never use. There are a huge sledgehammer, several sizes of nailing hammers, rubber-headed mallets, stone-carving and wood-carving hammers, and a few special purpose types. The kinds of hammers used for carpentry come in different weights. The usual weight is sixteen ounces. The slightly smaller 10-ounce size also comes in handy.

This is a common garden variety hammer, the kind most often used. It is sometimes called a claw hammer because the back end, which is used for pulling out nails, looks something like a two-fingered claw.

Efficient nailing doesn't require brute strength. As with sawing, it is the tool that should do the work—not a lot of muscle and sweat. Hold the hammer near the end and **swing** it! Don't push it. Let the weight and momentum of the steel head drive the nail into the wood.

Very often a nail will bend as you are hammering it in. This is particularly true of finishing nails and other thin nails. If this happens, pull out the nail and throw it away. Try again with a fresh nail in a different spot. Don't try to hammer another nail into the old hole. (The hole itself is probably crooked!)

This is **not** a recommended way to hammer nails!

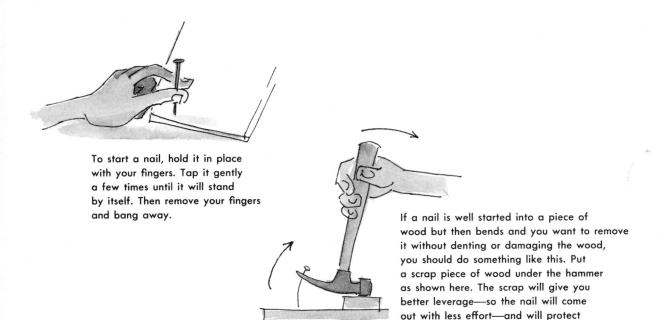

To start a nail, hold it in place with your fingers. Tap it gently a few times until it will stand by itself. Then remove your fingers and bang away.

If a nail is well started into a piece of wood but then bends and you want to remove it without denting or damaging the wood, you should do something like this. Put a scrap piece of wood under the hammer as shown here. The scrap will give you better leverage—so the nail will come out with less effort—and will protect your work from dents and scars.

All About Nails

The common nail is, as its name implies, the sort of nail you see most frequently. It is used in all kinds of general construction and varies in size from 20d (4 inches long) to 2d (about 1 inch long).

Nails are described in a strange, old-fashioned way. They were at one time sold by the hundred. One hundred 2-inch nails used to cost 6 pennies. So a 2-inch nail was —and still is—called a 6-penny nail! One hundred 3-inch nails used to cost 10 pennies. So a 3-inch nail was and is called a 10-penny nail. The abbreviation for penny is the letter d, from an old Roman coin called a denarius—an antique penny. So you will see nails described on the label on the box as 2d, or 10d, and so on. Most amateur woodworkers find all this mighty confusing. That's why when they buy nails, many people open up the box to see exactly what they are getting!

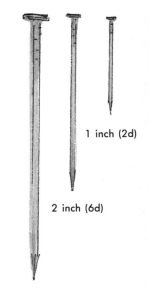

1 inch (2d)

2 inch (6d)

3 inch (10d)

Good judgment and a little common sense are necessary for any woodworking task. Try to find the right tool for each job. Use a lightweight hammer for thin, delicate nails, a heavy hammer for very large nails.

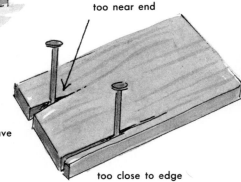

too near end

too close to edge

A nail that is placed too close to the end of a board, or very close to a side edge, will often cause the wood to split. This is particularly so if the nail is large. Try to keep the nail as far away from the edge as possible, even if you have to angle it in somewhat. Another way to avoid splits is to drill a hole where the nail is to go. This is especially useful when you are working with hardwoods such as maple or oak.

There are many specialized kinds of nails: for roofing, for hammering into cement, for holding cloth in place, for boat building, and so on. Nails that will be exposed to weather are given a rustproof coating. This process of coating the nail with zinc is called galvanizing. If you were going to build a bird house, or a backyard shed, you would want to use nails that wouldn't rust. The logical choice would be galvanized nails, which are available in all sizes.

Something like a boat, which would be around water all the time, should be made with nails or screws that won't rust—copper or bronze or galvanized steel nails.

3. Measuring, Drilling, and Planing

Measuring Tools

Measuring tools don't actually do any work themselves. But they are essential for getting parts that are the right size and that fit together properly. You can't tell how long a board is or how wide it is or where to cut it unless you have a measuring tool. What you need is either a folding ruler or a tape measure.

Some try squares, like the one discussed on page 8, have inch marks along the ruler edge and thus can be used for measuring short distances.

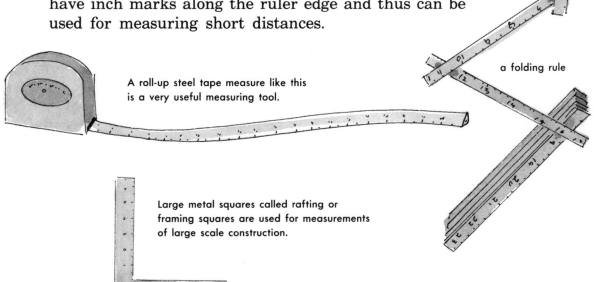

A roll-up steel tape measure like this is a very useful measuring tool.

a folding rule

Large metal squares called rafting or framing squares are used for measurements of large scale construction.

Drilling Holes

There will be many times when you will want to use a drill to make holes. For example, a preliminary hole is needed for any but the smallest screw. Holes are also needed when parts are attached by nut and bolt, and when dowels are used. You might also need a hole if you wanted to hammer a large nail into a hard wood like oak or maple.

The part of the drill that does the cutting is called a bit, or twist drill. It is fitted into the drill itself by means of a chuck. Here is how to put the bit into the drill: hold the handle of the drill so it won't move, then turn the chuck.

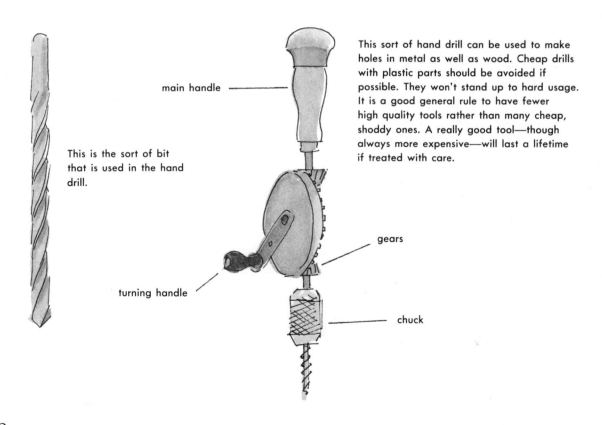

main handle

This is the sort of bit that is used in the hand drill.

This sort of hand drill can be used to make holes in metal as well as wood. Cheap drills with plastic parts should be avoided if possible. They won't stand up to hard usage. It is a good general rule to have fewer high quality tools rather than many cheap, shoddy ones. A really good tool—though always more expensive—will last a lifetime if treated with care.

gears

turning handle

chuck

Look inside the "mouth" of the chuck and you'll see that the jaws inside the chuck open and close, depending on which way the chuck is turned. Place the bit inside the chuck and then turn the chuck until the bit is firmly gripped. You are ready to drill.

The size of the hole is, of course, determined by the size of the bit you use. Here's how to go about it. Place a scrap piece of wood under the wood through which you are going to drill. The scrap is important. Without it you would get a jagged edge when the drill broke through, and you would drill a hole right into your work table.

Hold your wood down securely. If possible use a vise, a clamp, or an assistant to hold it so it won't wiggle about as you drill. Before starting to drill, make a dent with a nail or center punch at the place where the hole is to go.

As you work be careful to keep the drill straight up and down. Start slowly, checking continually that the drill is in a vertical position.

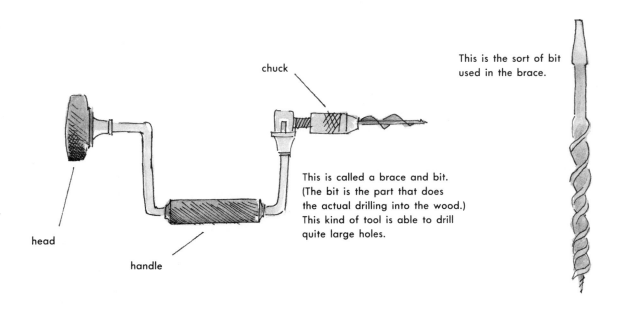

chuck

This is the sort of bit used in the brace.

This is called a brace and bit. (The bit is the part that does the actual drilling into the wood.) This kind of tool is able to drill quite large holes.

head

handle

Many homes have an electric drill, which is a useful thing to own. It works like a hand drill, except that the chuck is tightened by means of a little gearlike gadget called a key.

An electric drill uses the same kind of bit as a hand drill—but it can also be fitted with a bit like the one shown. This bit can drill a hole that is quite large—up to 2 inches in diameter.

An electric drill comes in handy for all sorts of woodworking operations. It is not difficult to use and is not much more expensive than a good hand drill. Instead of a bit, a sanding pad can be attached to it, which will make quick work out of tedious sanding jobs. Another attachment holds a soft polishing pad that will give waxed surfaces a high polish.

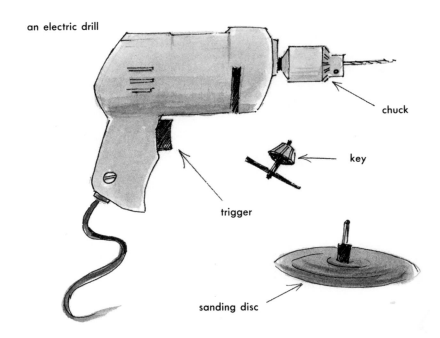

an electric drill

chuck

key

trigger

sanding disc

24

Some Other Tools

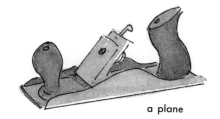

a plane

The plane is one of those traditional tools that you will find in the toolbox of every professional carpenter, and in a lot of home workshops. It shapes and smoothes wood by shaving off thin layers of it. But a plane is a tricky thing. It is difficult to adjust. And to use it effectively requires some practice and a properly sharpened blade.

A good substitute for the difficult-to-handle plane is the tool shown here. It is easy to use and acts a little like a coarse file or rasp. It has spaces between the cutting teeth through which wood shavings can escape. Because of these spaces the blade never clogs up. If the cutting edges get dull, the entire blade can be replaced. One of the trade names for this tool is "Surform."

A good sharp file is another useful tool. It will help you to round corners, get rid of bumps, and smooth rough edges. When a file has large, coarse teeth it is called a rasp. This tool can remove a surprising amount of wood

Files come in various sizes, shapes, and degrees of coarseness.

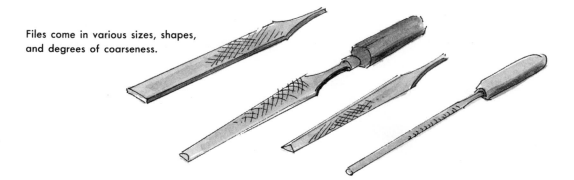

in little time. Files, rasps, and "Surform" tools work a little like a ripsaw. The cutting action is done on the *forward* stroke. There is not much accomplished by simply pushing and pulling these tools back and forth. What is needed is a steady, strong forward stroke, and a light back stroke. The wood you are working on should be held securely with a vise or clamp, so that you can use two hands on the tool and really bear down.

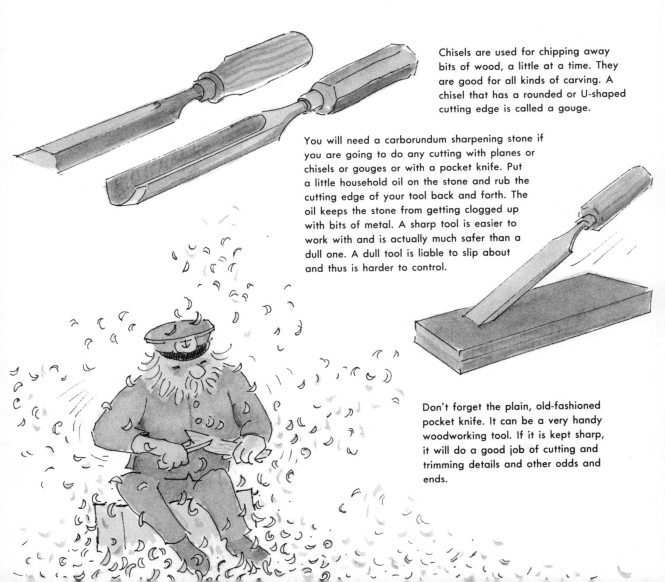

Chisels are used for chipping away bits of wood, a little at a time. They are good for all kinds of carving. A chisel that has a rounded or U-shaped cutting edge is called a gouge.

You will need a carborundum sharpening stone if you are going to do any cutting with planes or chisels or gouges or with a pocket knife. Put a little household oil on the stone and rub the cutting edge of your tool back and forth. The oil keeps the stone from getting clogged up with bits of metal. A sharp tool is easier to work with and is actually much safer than a dull one. A dull tool is liable to slip about and thus is harder to control.

Don't forget the plain, old-fashioned pocket knife. It can be a very handy woodworking tool. If it is kept sharp, it will do a good job of cutting and trimming details and other odds and ends.

4. All About Wood

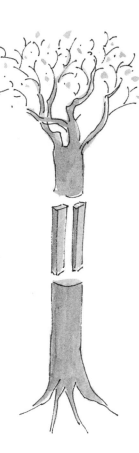

Like any material, there are things you can do with wood and things you can't do. Some shapes and forms are suitable for wood; others are not. For example, very thin structures that must be strong shouldn't be made out of wood. A very thin, delicate table would be better in metal than in wood. It wouldn't be very practical to make a typewriter out of wood either! Or how about a wood screwdriver! However, it is amazing just how many different objects can be built from wood if you use the right kind of wood and pay attention to the grain. This business of wood grain is of great importance.

Grain

As a tree grows the fibers of the wood form in a very definite way. The fibers run from the bottom up. And it is these fibers that make up the grain. You might think of a wood board as being like a bundle of uncooked spaghetti! Each piece of spaghetti in the bundle is like a fiber in the wood.

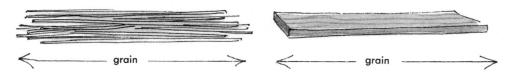

← ———— grain ————→   ← ———— grain ————→

If you look at a wood board, you will see that there seem to be lines running from one end to the other.

grain

If you look at the end of the board, you will see a completely different pattern—a tight, dense one. (This would be the end view of our bundle of spaghetti.) Of course, there are exceptions to the rule, depending on the kind of wood and how the tree was cut up into boards.

Because of the grain, wood is strong in some ways and not in others. When the grain of a piece of wood runs from one end to another, as in the illustration on the left below, the board will be relatively strong. If the grain runs from side to side, as shown on the right, the board will break more easily. Think of our bundle of spaghetti again, with all the pieces lightly glued together. It would

This arrangement of spaghetti, with short pieces, would be very weak.

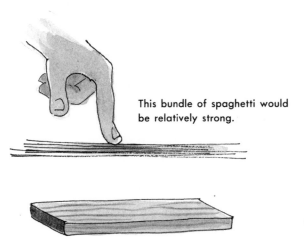

This bundle of spaghetti would be relatively strong.

be fairly difficult to break it in half. Then think of another bundle made of very short pieces of spaghetti. It wouldn't take much effort to snap this bundle apart. The grain of wood acts very much like this.

If you have a small scrap of wood available, try wedging up one end and hitting the middle with a hammer. Notice the way in which the wood breaks. A little experimenting like this will demonstrate clearly just how wood grain affects strength.

Grain is also important when it comes to shaping and cutting. You will find it is quite difficult to work on the end of a board. The grain on the end of a board is called end grain and can't be whittled or chiseled or sanded as easily as the grain that runs along the side of the board.

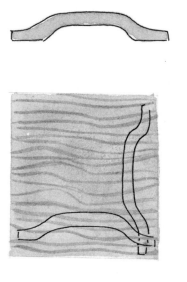

Let's see how this business of grain works in an actual situation. Suppose you wanted to make a handle for a toolbox, and you had a square piece of wood to make it out of. If the shape of the handle was to be as shown, how would you cut it out? The right way would be to have the wood grain running the long way— from one end of the handle to the other. If the grain ran from the top to the bottom, a sudden yank or bang would probably break the handle.

Lumber

The most common sort of wood—and the kind that is used for most of the projects described later in the book —is pine. It is stocked by all lumberyards. The ordinary pine board will be 1 inch thick and anywhere from 2 to 12 inches wide.

If you go to a lumberyard to buy a few boards, you should know ahead of time just what to ask for. If you simply ask for a "wood board," there is no telling what you will get. You should know what size board you want —and what kind of wood.

If you wanted a board that was 1 inch thick and 6 inches wide, you would ask for a 1 by 6. If you wanted a board 2 inches thick and 8 inches wide, you would ask for a 2 by 8. And you would also have to say what length board you needed. You might ask for 8 feet of 1 by 6, for example.

Heavy wood, the kind used for building houses or for making table legs, or whenever a lot of strength is needed, is called construction lumber. Sizes such as 2 by 4, or 2 by 8, or 4 by 4 fit into this category. The wood is often fir or spruce or some other locally available wood, and it isn't usually as smooth or as neat looking as pine.

Lumber sizes are tricky in that the size you ask for is not what you get! The sizes given are for rough, unfinished lumber. The wood you get from the lumberyard is smooth. It has been run through a planing machine to remove the rough surfaces. This smoothing operation reduces the size of the board somewhat. So that the 1 by 4 you buy will be approximately ¾ inch by 3¾ inches. The 1 by 6 will actually be about ¾ inch by 5¾ inches, and so on.

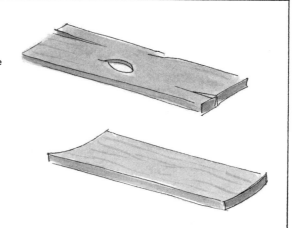

What you want to avoid when choosing lumber are boards that are warped or cracked or that have large, loose knot holes. Small knot holes won't seriously weaken wood construction and actually will often add a little interest and variety to a finished piece. If you give the matter a little thought, you can manage to cut up your lumber so that the knot holes don't end up at an unwanted location, such as on an edge or corner.

There are two grades of pine. The best grade is called "clear." This means that the wood has no knotholes. The most often used pine is called "number two." It has knotholes of various sizes, which are usually not big enough to cause any problems. Clear pine costs two or three times as much as number two pine and is used when you are terribly fussy or when cost is no consideration.

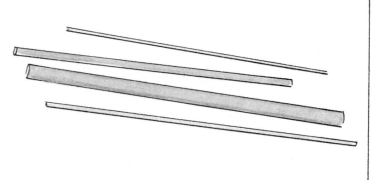

Another kind of wood you will sometimes need are dowels. These are simply straight hardwood rods. They come in various diameters from ⅛ inch up to 1 inch and are sold in 3-foot lengths. Hardware stores, as well as lumberyards, carry them.

Plywood

A lot of the wood used in general construction is plywood. It comes in large panels, usually 4 feet by 8 feet, and in various thicknesses. It is a wonderful material where a large area of wood is needed. Walls, table tops, cabinets, and doors are often made from plywood.

The trouble with plywood is that the edges have a rather rough look and must be carefully sanded or filed to get a nice finish. It is also rather difficult to saw because the edges have a tendency to splinter unless power tools are used.

Plywood is available in thicknesses of ¼ inch up to 1 inch. It can also be had with many different surfaces. For example, it is possible to get a piece of plywood with the top layer made of a very expensive and fancy wood, such as teak or walnut.

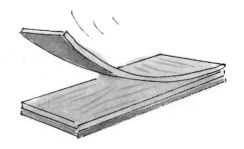

Plywood is made of various layers of very thin wood positioned so that the grain of each layer runs in a different direction from the layer next to it. If the grain of one layer ran up and down, the grain of the next layer would run back and forth. The next would run up and down, and so on for as many layers as there are. All of the layers are glued together. This results in a strong piece of wood that won't ever split.

Beautiful Wood

The kind of wood you are likely to find in a scrap pile or left over from a construction job will—aside from plywood—be either pine or fir. Fir is used a great deal in house construction. The 2 by 4s that hold up the walls of frame houses are usually fir. It has a more pronounced grain than pine and isn't quite as light in color. It isn't usually made into the kind of boards you'll need for the projects described later in the book.

When pine is sanded smooth and finished off in one of the ways mentioned on the next page, it can have a lovely appearance—particularly if the pattern of the grain is nice.

But there are as many other kinds of wood as there are different kinds of trees. As you become experienced working with wood and skilled in the use of power tools, and as you begin to make more elaborate projects, you will want to try some of these woods. Many lumberyards carry only pine, fir, and plywood. But if you ask around, you will find some yards that carry a larger variety of woods, such as walnut, mahogany, maple, redwood, oak, and even teak, cherry, larch, pear, ebony, and chestnut.

Some of these woods are a good deal harder than pine. You'll want to use a sharp saw and work carefully. But they are worth the trouble and the extra money because all of them have beautiful coloring and a pattern to the grain that is often quite elegant.

5. Finishing Wood

If you want your woodworking project to look really good —and, of course, you do—you must take the time to finish it off properly. Your work will look sloppy if there are ragged edges, splintered corners, and rough surfaces.

The first thing to do is to make sure all the nails are flush with the surface of the wood.

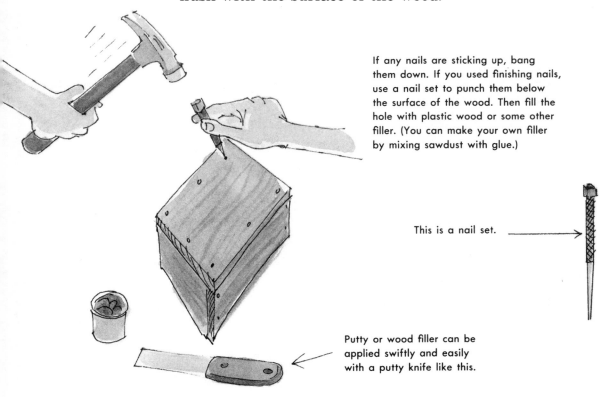

If any nails are sticking up, bang them down. If you used finishing nails, use a nail set to punch them below the surface of the wood. Then fill the hole with plastic wood or some other filler. (You can make your own filler by mixing sawdust with glue.)

This is a nail set. ⟶

Putty or wood filler can be applied swiftly and easily with a putty knife like this.

The next thing to do is to sandpaper the wood all over. Sandpaper comes in different grades: rough, medium, and fine. If the wood you used is scarred and splintered and dirty, you should start with the rough grade of sandpaper, then proceed to the medium, and end up with the fine.

Sandpaper works best, and is easiest to handle, if folded and cut and arranged as shown below. This way one rough surface doesn't rub against another, wearing away both uselessly. When one part of the sandpaper is worn out, you can rearrange the quarters to get the use of a fresh part. Simply ripping off an odd piece of sandpaper and using it without a back-up block is inefficient—and sandpaper is not inexpensive.

A back-up block is simply a small, rectangular block of wood around which the sandpaper is wrapped. A good size is 2½ inches by 4 inches by ¾ inch thick. It should be used as often as possible because it keeps the paper bearing down evenly, giving you a better finish. A small piece of sandpaper held in the fingers will accentuate the "hills" and "valleys" in the wood.

After the wood has been sanded as smooth as possible there are a number of different things you can do to complete the finishing job. If you like the way the wood itself looks, you can simply rub on some floor or furniture wax. This will help to keep the wood from getting dirty and will give it a nice, shiny finish.

Another possibility is to paint on a coat or two of either shellac or varnish. Shellac and varnish, as well as wax and paint, serve to seal the pores of the wood. This keeps out moisture and prevents dirt from working into the surface of the wood. You'll find that any wood that has been left unfinished will, in time, take on a scruffy, dirty look.

If the wood doesn't please you in its natural state, or if you are fond of bright colors, you can paint it. Before applying the paint, however, you should give the wood a coat of shellac. This is particularly important if there are any knotholes. Without shellac the knotholes will show through the paint and spoil what would otherwise be a smooth and even coating.

Some people like to finish off a wood surface by staining. Stain is not a protective coating. It is just a way to change the color of wood. It will also usually make the grain more noticeable. Stain can be had in various mixtures. Some stains will give a piece of pine the color of mahogany or walnut or oak. Paint stores usually have samples of wood finished with different kinds of stains so that you can see what you are going to get. After the stain has been applied, the usual thing is to put on a final coat of varnish or wax.

When varnishing or shellacking or painting, it is important to avoid dust. Use a brush to get rid of any dust or dirt left over from your sandpapering, or wipe off the wood with a clean rag that has a little turpentine on it. If you paint or varnish over a dirty or dusty surface, you won't get a smooth, glossy finish.

Don't forget to clean your brushes when you are through. This is a big bother, but it must be done if you are going to use the brushes again. Use the proper solvent for whatever you applied. The solvent for shellac is alcohol. For water-based paint, it is water. For oil-based paint, it is turpentine. Read the label on the can.

One way to avoid messing around with brushes and having to clean them is to use paint that comes in an

aerosol can. If you apply the paint in many thin layers, you will get nice even color. Follow the directions on the can. The only disadvantage to this way of painting is the cost. A plain can of paint will cost a good deal less than an aerosol spray can and will last a lot longer.

6. Planning Your Project

With very simple projects you can sometimes just grab your tools and a piece of wood and get right to work. If you were making a little box or a pair of bookends, for instance, you might be able to get by in this way. But for anything more complicated you should have at least a rough plan. A plan will help you to visualize the finished job. It will tell you what materials you will need—what size lumber, what kind of nails, and so on. And it will help you to cut out and assemble the pieces in a logical sequence.

You don't have to know anything about drawing to make a working plan. The plan can be very rough if the project is a simple one. If it's complicated, you should take the time and trouble to draw more careful plans. A few sample plans are shown below.

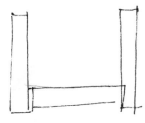

A very rough sketch like this might be all you would need if you were going to make something as simple as the book rack shown here. None of the sizes are critical. As long as both sides fitted up against the bottom you would be all right.

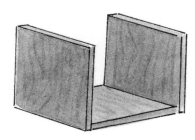

If you want to be more careful, you can make
plans like this, in which you work out
ahead of time exactly what sizes are needed.

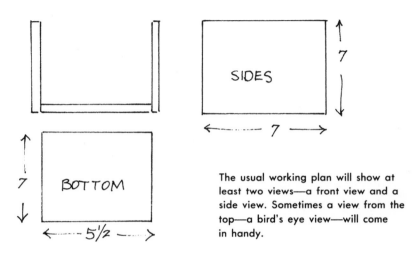

The usual working plan will show at
least two views—a front view and a
side view. Sometimes a view from the
top—a bird's eye view—will come
in handy.

A sketch like this not only gives
sizes but a picture of what the
finished job will look like.

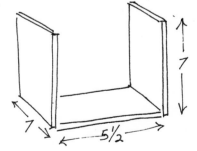

In any plan it is important to indicate
the sizes. You can do this as shown
simply by drawing an arrow and writing
in the distance from end to end—or
from side to side.

If you want to do a really professional job of planning, you can make what is called a scale drawing. This means that the plan is in proper proportion to the actual finished job.

In a *full-scale* (or full-size) drawing, for example, a piece of wood that was to be 2 inches long would be drawn on your paper 2 inches long. If you didn't have a big enough piece of paper, or if your project was very large, you could reduce the scale by half. Then the 2-inch-long board would be 1 inch long on your drawing.

You could also work to a smaller scale, making 2 inches equal to ½ inch or ¼ inch. However, this sort of precise planning requires particular tools—it is known as mechanical drawing. It is a specialized field and not our concern here.

When a construction is complicated, the parts are sometimes separated, as in the drawing of this cart, or spaced apart, in order to make the plan more understandable.

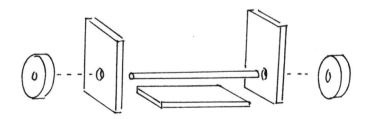

Drawn plans like these are really a form of language. They can explain something more clearly than the written or spoken word.

7. Some Easy-To-Build Woodworking Projects

A Checkerboard

A checkerboard is a good beginning project because it requires no complicated operations—just a good deal of sawing, sandpapering, and gluing.

The best wood to use for a checkerboard is lattice wood, a thin wood—it is ¼ inch thick—that comes in various widths and is available from most lumberyards. You will need 12 feet of this kind of wood, 2 inches wide. If you can't find lattice wood, you can use 1 by 2 inch wood. This is considerably thicker and will make a heavier checkerboard, but otherwise will be perfectly all right. If you happen to have another kind of wood of similar size, you can use it, or you may be able to get somebody who has power tools to cut up some strips for you. You will also need a piece of plywood (any thickness) about 16 by 16 inches onto which the checkerboard squares will be glued.

Start by cutting your wood into squares. Measure the width of the strip you are using. Even if you bought some stripping that was supposed to be 2 inches wide, you will probably find it is actually about 1¾ inches wide. (Re-

Because this checkerboard is the first
project, it is described in much greater
detail than the projects that follow.

member that the size of the wood is usually a little less
than described because it will have been planed down at
the sawmill.) If the wood measures 1¾ inches wide you
will, of course, have to cut it into 1¾-inch lengths to get
your squares. Here's how to do it.

Caution: If the end of the wood strip is
split or damaged in any way, cut off the
bad part.

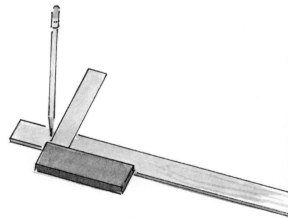

1. Make a mark 1¾ inches from the end
of the strip.

2. Using your try square, draw a line
through the mark and across the wood.

44

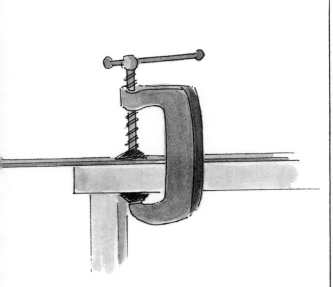

3. Hold the wood down firmly, in a vise, or with a "C" clamp, or with your foot, or with the help of a friend.

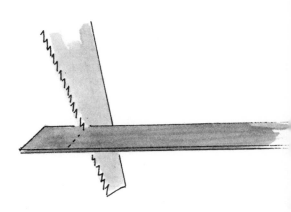

4. Cut along the line. Be sure to hold the small piece that is being cut off so that it won't split away when the saw completes the cut, leaving you with a splintered edge. If you use a cross-cut saw with rough teeth, you may find that you get a rather jagged cut. See if you can find a smaller saw with smaller teeth. Or use a hacksaw.

5. Place a sheet of sandpaper (medium or fine grade) on a smooth, flat surface. Then rub the square you've just cut back and forth across it to remove the rough edges.

6. Continue cutting and sanding until you have 64 squares. This will give your arm a good work out! But don't get impatient and rush or you will end up with a sloppy looking board.

7. Stain 32 of the squares a dark brown. If you don't have stain, you can use paint. The other 32 squares can be left untouched or finished in a lighter color.

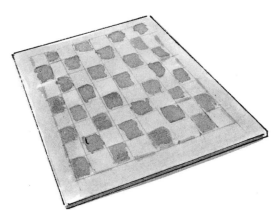

8. After the finish has dried, temporarily assemble the squares on a flat surface. Check to see that everything looks all right. Then measure one side of the board. (If your squares are 1¾ inches, the length of each side would be 14 inches. If your squares are 1 inch, the length of each side would be 8 inches.)

9. You will need a piece of plywood onto which the squares will be glued. The plywood should be an inch or two larger all around than the assembled squares. If the length of your assembled squares was 14 inches, then your plywood should be about 16 by 16 inches. Cut the plywood to the required size. Sand the edges.

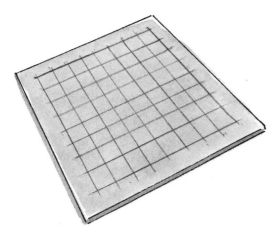

10. Place the squares on the plywood and mark their location with ruled pencil lines. If you don't do this and just start gluing down the squares, there is a good chance the squares will go off at an angle.

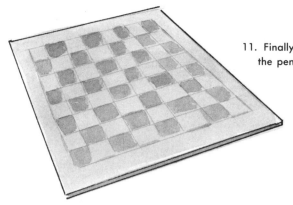

11. Finally, glue down the squares using the pencil lines as your guide.

If you happen to need a set of checkers, you can make them yourself from a thick wood pole— a mop or broom handle would do. Saw off 16 one-half-inch thick slices. Paint or stain half of them a dark color, and you are ready to play.

A Toolbox

When you have to take your tools somewhere to do an on-the-spot bit of carpentry, you must have a way of carrying them. A toolbox is the answer. The toolbox can also be a way of storing your tools, neatly and conveniently. Tossing a batch of tools into a cardboard box or piling them up at the back of your workbench is very unprofessional. It is also bad for the tools. The sharp steel edges of chisels, saws, and files get dulled when they bump into and rub up against one another.

The toolbox shown here is a simple, open, traylike container with a few compartments. What makes it special is the large carrying handle. The wood for this must be chosen with care because the handle will have to support a good deal of weight. A piece of 1 by 3 pine will do the trick, but make sure it doesn't have any knotholes or splits. Several other possibilities for the handle, using other materials, are shown in the drawings below.

The handle of this toolbox is a piece of 1 by 3 inch board. Use a file and sandpaper to round off the edges of the board.

You can use a sturdy pole to make the handle for the toolbox. A heavy dowel or a piece of broomstick will do the trick nicely.

The bottom and sides of the toolbox are simply three pieces of board nailed securely together.

This is the shape to make the end pieces if you are going to use a pole handle. The hole must, of course, be the right size for the pole.

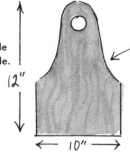

12"

10"

Use a scroll saw or else a file to get these curves.

The sizes given here are only suggested sizes. You should modify these dimensions to suit your needs and the materials you have to work with. Decide on just what tools are going to go into the toolbox before you make any final decisions.

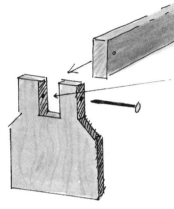

If you are going to make your toolbox with a 1 by 3 inch board handle, you will have to cut a notch like this.

Don't hammer in a nail to secure the handle. The wood might split. Instead, drill a hole through the end piece and the handle. Then insert a piece of steel rod or a heavy nail. A little glue or cement will keep the rod or nail from coming out.

If you want to use a rod handle but can't drill suitable holes, you might use an arrangement like this. A strip of metal is bent over the rod and attached with nails or screws.

Punch holes in the strap.

metal strap
(Heavy leather could be used instead.)

30"

If all else fails, you can fall back on this simple method: Pass a heavy piece of rope through holes in the end pieces and then knot the rope as shown.

A Storage Cabinet

Everybody needs some kind of storage cabinet. Depending on its size and proportions, it can serve many purposes. It can be designed to hold books—in which case it would really be a small bookcase. Or it can be designed to hold bills, household records, and other papers. In the kitchen it can hold spices. In the shop it can be a holder for nuts and bolts and screws or small tools. It can provide a safe storage as well as a display place for model cars and trains or a rock collection.

Building a storage cabinet may sound like a pretty difficult undertaking. But it isn't. A storage cabinet is really no more than a box with a shelf or two in it. And as with any piece of carpentry, you can end up with a neat, good-looking job, or a rough and sloppy one—depending on how careful you are and how much trouble you take with measuring, cutting, fitting, and finishing.

Here is an "exploded" view of a cabinet with one shelf. The sizes given are for a cabinet that would be suitable for storing books—in other words, a bookcase.

The back of the cabinet can be ¼-inch plywood.

The lumber used is 1 inch by 8 inches. (Remember, the finished size of the board will be ¾ by 7¼ inches.)

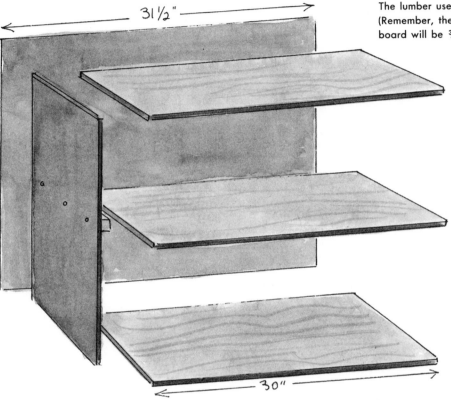

31½"

7¼"

21"

30"

Make the shelf slightly shorter than the top and bottom pieces if you want it to be removable.

These strips of wood support the shelf. Hold them in place with glue and screws, or glue and nails.

If you make a cabinet like this out of plywood rather than board, you will have to very carefully sandpaper the edges that show.

If you want to make a tall bookcase, you can follow the arrangement shown here. Simply lengthen the side pieces and add more shelves. In fact, if you want, you can make a bookcase that goes from floor to ceiling.

The drawings below show several different cabinet arrangements. What you should do first is decide exactly what is going to go into your cabinet. Then work out for yourself the size and shelf arrangement that best serves your purpose.

A variety of partitions can be used to divide the interior into spaces you have a particular need for. A cabinet like this would be nice over a desk. You could keep letters, stationery, pencils, stamps, and whatnot in neat order.

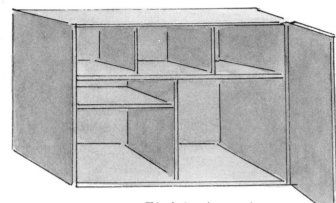

This design shows a door, which you may or may not want to add.

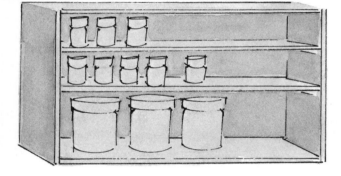

A small cabinet with shelves that are placed close together makes a good place to store spices and seasonings. If the space in your kitchen is limited, you can choose a size and proportion that best fits the available room.

A cabinet or bookcase is best assembled with the wood on the floor. After the top, bottom, and two sides are nailed together, attach the back. The back helps to hold everything together, making a rigid "box."

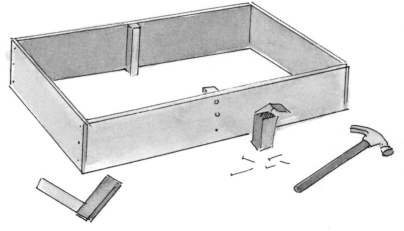

Here is a display cabinet. It is just the thing for storing various kinds of collections—rocks and minerals, or model cars, or coins, or fossils, or whatever you happen to have that you want to display in a really nice way.

The shelves are made of glass, and a light bulb is hidden in the top of this cabinet.

A piece of board across the top will hide the bare light bulb and the socket into which it is screwed.

Shelves of glass rather than wood are used so that the light can reach the items displayed on the lower shelves.

A base like this is not really essential but will improve the appearance of the cabinet.

A Weather Vane

A weather vane is a practical device that will tell you from which direction the wind is blowing. While a weather expert can make certain predictions with this knowledge, for most people wind direction is not an exactly vital bit of information. But a weather vane is worth building anyhow because it will make a good-looking addition to a rooftop . . . or if you don't have a rooftop to put it on, it makes a nice inside decoration. You can mount your weather vane on a wall or perch it on a corner of a desk or bookcase.

All sorts of subject matter has been used for weather vanes. If the owner of a house was a former sea captain, the chances are his weather vane would be in the form of a ship. A dairy farmer might have a cow weather vane on the roof of his barn. Some antique weather vanes were in the form of horses, fish, Indians, roosters, and even giant grasshoppers.

The trick in getting a weather vane to work properly is in the balance. It must have equal weight on both sides of the pivot point. At the same time, one side must offer more resistance to the force of the wind than the other side. The drawings below explain how this works.

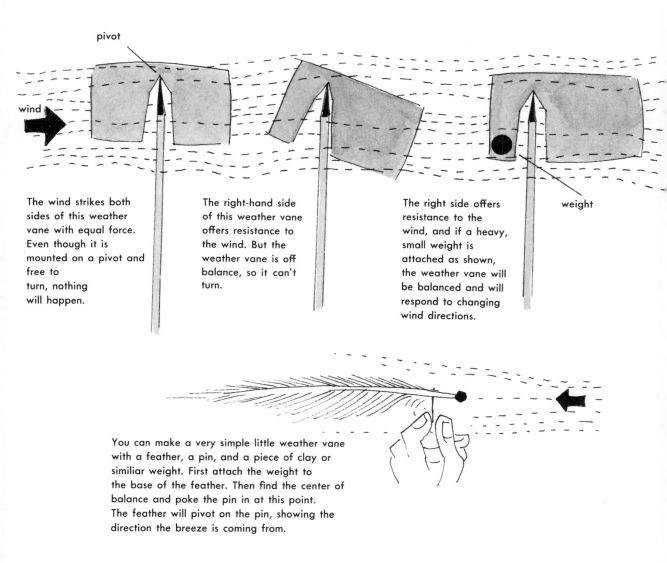

pivot

wind

weight

The wind strikes both sides of this weather vane with equal force. Even though it is mounted on a pivot and free to turn, nothing will happen.

The right-hand side of this weather vane offers resistance to the wind. But the weather vane is off balance, so it can't turn.

The right side offers resistance to the wind, and if a heavy, small weight is attached as shown, the weather vane will be balanced and will respond to changing wind directions.

You can make a very simple little weather vane with a feather, a pin, and a piece of clay or similiar weight. First attach the weight to the base of the feather. Then find the center of balance and poke the pin in at this point. The feather will pivot on the pin, showing the direction the breeze is coming from.

A whale weather vane, like the one shown, on page 55, can be made from a 1-foot length of 1 by 8 inch board. The other materials you'll need are a block of wood for the base and a stiff rod about 10 inches long. You'll also need some kind of weight to get the balance right. A 10-ounce fisherman's lead sinker should do the trick.

First draw the outline of the whale on the wood and then cut it out with a coping saw. (A coping saw, as explained on page 13, will be able to follow the curved lines with ease.)

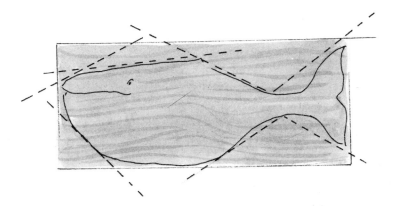

If you don't have a coping saw, you can rough out the whale with several straight cuts. This will remove the great bulk of wood. Then you can finish up with a rasp or file or Surform tool, or even a whittling knife

Be careful of the fins. The grain isn't running in the ideal direction here, and rough handling could knock off the tips.

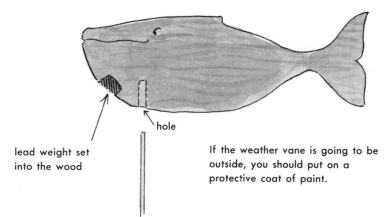

Drill a hole for the rod on which the weather vane pivots. Make sure the whale pivots freely. The top of the rod should be rounded and sanded smooth. A little soap on the rod will act as a lubricant.

lead weight set into the wood

hole

If the weather vane is going to be outside, you should put on a protective coat of paint.

If you live in a building without an available roof or backyard, you will have to settle for an indoor weather vane. In this case, you can use a ⅜-inch wood dowel for the rod. If you happen to live in a house where you can mount the weather vane on the roof, you will want to use a brass or aluminum rod instead of a dowel. (A wood rod might break in a gale, and a steel rod would rust.) Get some experienced help to figure out some way of attaching the rod to the roof. Garage or shed roofs are good places for a weather vane. It is even possible to mount a weather vane on a tall pole stuck in the ground, or on a fence.

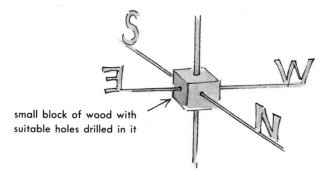

small block of wood with suitable holes drilled in it

If you want to add the compass points to the lower part of your weather vane, you can make an arrangement like this. The letters can be cut out of wood or metal, or they can be bought ready-made at most any large hardware store.

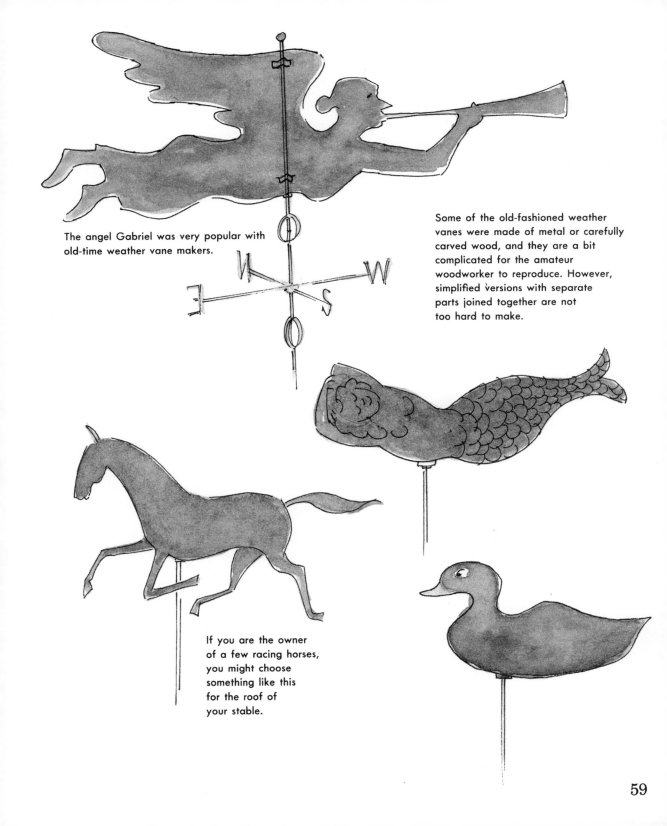

The angel Gabriel was very popular with old-time weather vane makers.

Some of the old-fashioned weather vanes were made of metal or carefully carved wood, and they are a bit complicated for the amateur woodworker to reproduce. However, simplified versions with separate parts joined together are not too hard to make.

If you are the owner of a few racing horses, you might choose something like this for the roof of your stable.

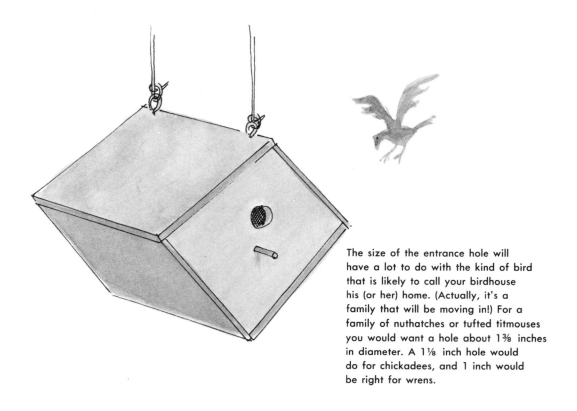

The size of the entrance hole will have a lot to do with the kind of bird that is likely to call your birdhouse his (or her) home. (Actually, it's a family that will be moving in!) For a family of nuthatches or tufted titmouses you would want a hole about 1⅜ inches in diameter. A 1⅛ inch hole would do for chickadees, and 1 inch would be right for wrens.

A Birdhouse

A birdhouse like this is an easy project, and it will make a snug home for a bird family. It is basically a square box, suspended from one edge. The size will be determined by the kind of bird you would like to have move in. A house for a wren, for example, which is a rather small bird, would be much smaller than one for a bluebird.

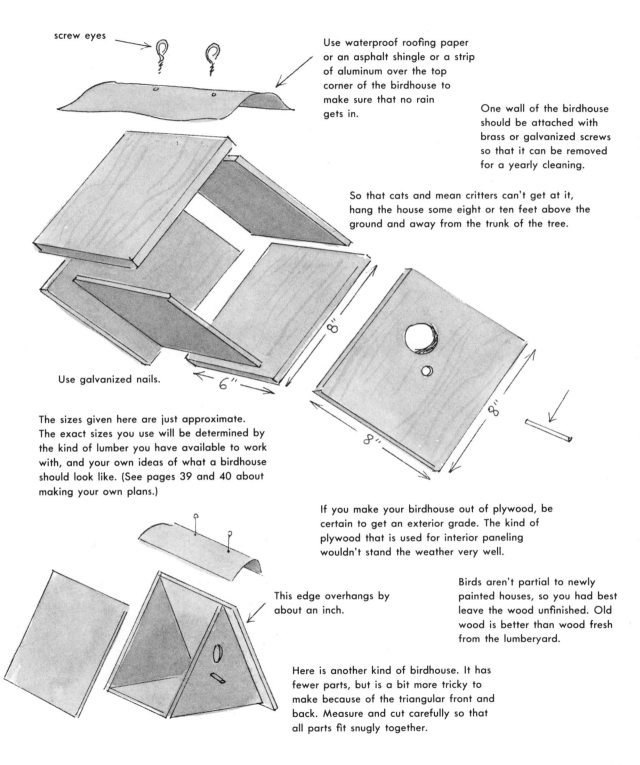

screw eyes

Use waterproof roofing paper or an asphalt shingle or a strip of aluminum over the top corner of the birdhouse to make sure that no rain gets in.

One wall of the birdhouse should be attached with brass or galvanized screws so that it can be removed for a yearly cleaning.

So that cats and mean critters can't get at it, hang the house some eight or ten feet above the ground and away from the trunk of the tree.

8"

Use galvanized nails.

6"

8"

8"

The sizes given here are just approximate. The exact sizes you use will be determined by the kind of lumber you have available to work with, and your own ideas of what a birdhouse should look like. (See pages 39 and 40 about making your own plans.)

If you make your birdhouse out of plywood, be certain to get an exterior grade. The kind of plywood that is used for interior paneling wouldn't stand the weather very well.

This edge overhangs by about an inch.

Birds aren't partial to newly painted houses, so you had best leave the wood unfinished. Old wood is better than wood fresh from the lumberyard.

Here is another kind of birdhouse. It has fewer parts, but is a bit more tricky to make because of the triangular front and back. Measure and cut carefully so that all parts fit snugly together.

A Treasure Chest with a Secret Compartment

The bottom part of this chest is a simple box that is built in much the same way as the storage cabinet and toolbox already described. But the top, or lid, where the secret compartment is contained, is a little more tricky.

The two side pieces and the bottom of the lid are made first. Then some thin strips of wood are nailed onto the curved edges of the side pieces. However, not *all* of the wood strips are nailed down. Two of the strips look as though they are nailed in place, but actually they can be slid off to the side, opening up the secret compartment.

You can cut the thin strips of wood from a plank, but it will take a little patience. Perhaps you know somebody with power tools who will cut up the strips for you. Another possibility is to go to a lumberyard and buy some square molding. You will need about eight feet of the ¾ inch by ¾ inch size.

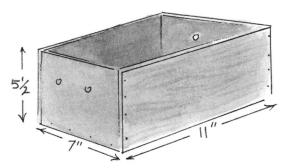

The bottom of the treasure chest is simply a box with holes drilled in the side pieces. The holes are for the rope handles.

5½

7"

11"

This is the bottom of the lid and the two side pieces.

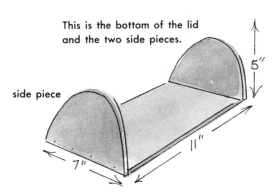

side piece

5"

11"

7"

The sizes given here—like most of the sizes given in this book—are just suggested ones. Decide what treasures you are going to put in your chest, then make your plans accordingly. If you are making a treasure chest in which you will store your collection of diamonds, you probably don't need a very large chest. If, on the other hand, you want to store your collection of volley balls, something a little larger might be what's needed!

Cut strips of wood to size.

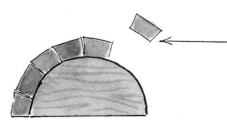

Before you put the wood strips in place, file or plane down their lower edges in order to get a wedge shape. This will let the strips fit together more closely.

Nail all but two of the strips onto the side pieces. Use 1¼ inch long finishing nails. Finishing nails are thin, so there is less danger of the wood splitting.

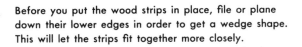

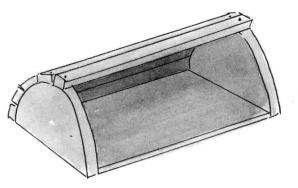

In order to make these two movable strips look like all the others, you will have to drive nails into the ends of each strip. Do this before the strips are in position on the lid. Then with a hacksaw or file, cut off the part of the nail that projects through the wood. You will end up with a short piece of nail that goes into the wood, but doesn't come out the other side. The nail won't serve any purpose, but nobody but you will know that.

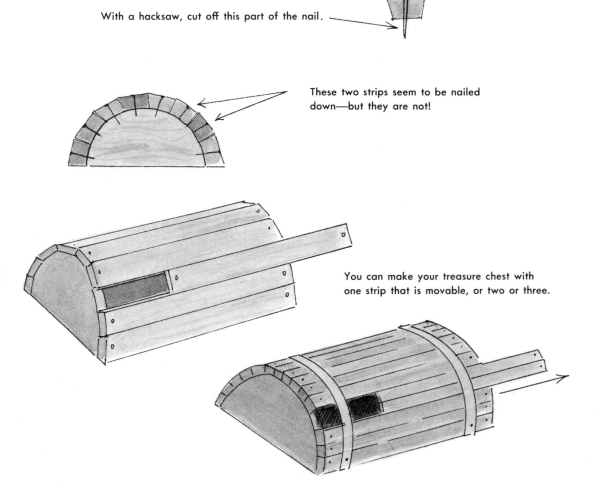

With a hacksaw, cut off this part of the nail.

These two strips seem to be nailed down—but they are not!

You can make your treasure chest with one strip that is movable, or two or three.

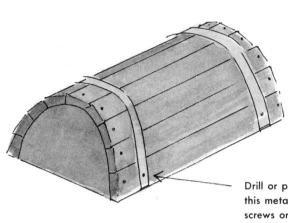

For the sake of clarity, these drawings show a rather wide strip of wood. In actual practice you will get a much better looking treasure chest if you use fairly narrow strips of wood—¾ by ¾ inch is a good size.

Drill or punch a hole near the ends of this metal reinforcing strip so that screws or nails can be used to fasten it in place.

A pair of hinges on the back will let the lid swing open. A hasp will enable you to keep the lid closed tight with a padlock.

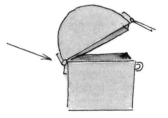

Any thin metal can be used to make the straps that are fastened on top of the wood strips. Brass straps look very nice. If you can't get brass, steel or aluminum will do. If you can't get metal of any kind, you may be able to find some heavy, stiff leather.

A Record Holder

If you own more than a few phonograph records, you may have a problem keeping them neatly stored and easily accessible. The record holder shown here is simple to make and will take care of your storage problem.

All you need to build it is one piece of 1 inch by 8 inch board 2 feet long, and six wire coat hangers. The hangers that cleaners put coats and jackets on vary from one shop to another. Some hangers have a cardboard tube instead of wire along the bottom. These are of no use here. And some hangers are made from wire that is thin and bends easily. They won't do either. But if you rummage around in the closets in your home—or the closets of friends and relatives—you should be able to find a few hangers of the right kind.

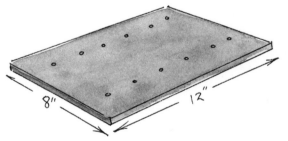

The first thing to do is sandpaper the wood until it is smooth and pleasant to the touch. Then drill the holes for the wire. A $\frac{1}{16}$ inch bit should give you a hole that will make a snug fit for most types of stiff hanger wire.

The holes should be approximately 1¼ inches apart.

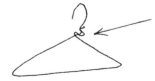

Cut off the twisted hook part of the hanger with a hacksaw. Straighten out the wire. Then cut a piece about 16 inches long, bend it into a loop, and insert it into the holes that were drilled into the base.

If the wire doesn't fit snugly, use some glue to hold it in place.

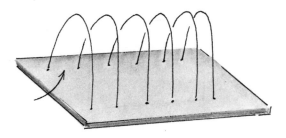

If you can't find any suitable wire, you can make a record holder like the one shown here using wood dowels. (Page 31 has some information about dowels.) The dowels should be ⅜ inch or ½ inch in diameter and about 8 inches long. You will, of course, have to drill a hole that is the right size for the dowels you are using.

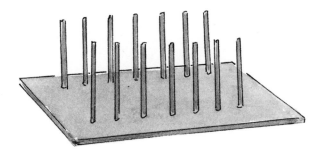

A Workbench

A good, sturdy workbench is a mighty nice thing to have. You can use it while you saw or hammer or chisel or finish wood, and you don't have to worry about mussing up a good chair or desk, or getting paint or varnish on the floor. And it can, of course, be used not only for woodworking but for all kinds of miscellaneous projects.

If you can find the room for a workbench, and if you can get the lumber, you should make one at the first opportunity. A workbench is fairly large and will take some time to build. But there are no tricky details or difficult operations.

The sizes given in the drawings are only approximate, because the size of your workbench will depend on where

The heavier and more rugged a workbench is, the better. Thick legs, a heavy top, and adequate bracing will make a good, sturdy place on which to work.

you can put it and what materials you have to work with. If, for example, you happen to have a nice, thick, strong piece of plywood that measures 3 feet by 4 feet, it's quite likely that the top of the table you build will end up being 3 feet by 4 feet!

You should also adjust the height of the table to suit you. Thirty inches is a good average height. But if you are very tall, add an inch or two. If you are short, lower the table two or three inches.

Plywood makes a good table top if it is smooth and of a heavy weight. The ¾-inch thickness is best. However, you can also use heavy boards placed next to one another.

The table can be fastened together with nails and glue, or screws, but you will get a more rugged table if you use nuts and bolts in the places that will be subject to heavy stress. Nuts and bolts are a little more trouble to work with and they are not inexpensive. But a workbench takes a lot of abuse, and you won't like it much if it starts wobbling and sagging after it has been in use for a while.

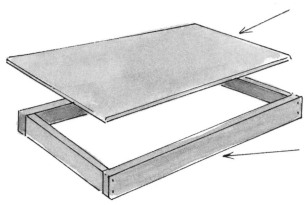

If you are using plywood for the top, cut it to suit the frame. (Or else make the frame to suit the plywood!)

The frame for the table top is made first. Use either 1 by 3 inch or 1 by 4 inch board.

If you are using planks of wood instead of plywood for the top, cut them to size first. Then make the frame to suit.

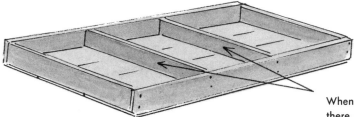

When planks are used instead of plywood, there should be additional support for the table top. The two additional boards shown here will serve this purpose. This drawing shows the table top turned upside down.

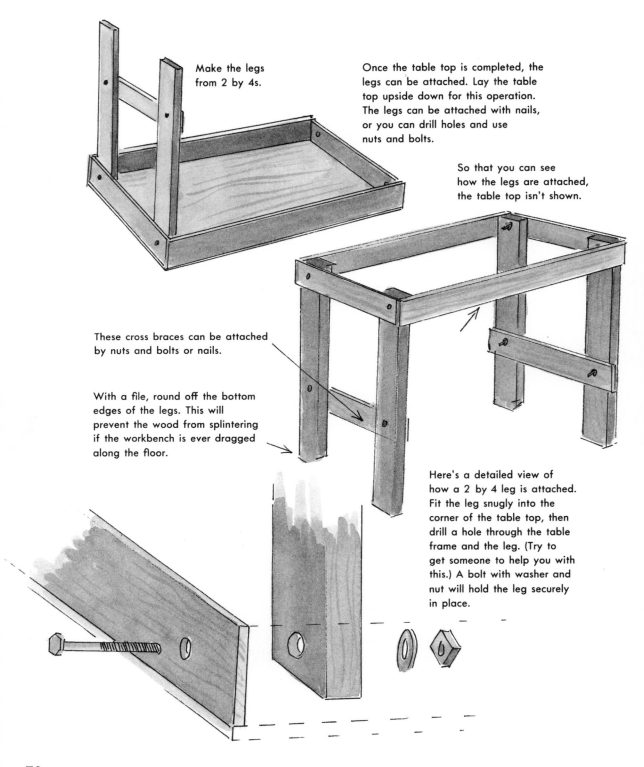

Make the legs
from 2 by 4s.

Once the table top is completed, the
legs can be attached. Lay the table
top upside down for this operation.
The legs can be attached with nails,
or you can drill holes and use
nuts and bolts.

So that you can see
how the legs are attached,
the table top isn't shown.

These cross braces can be attached
by nuts and bolts or nails.

With a file, round off the bottom
edges of the legs. This will
prevent the wood from splintering
if the workbench is ever dragged
along the floor.

Here's a detailed view of
how a 2 by 4 leg is attached.
Fit the leg snugly into the
corner of the table top, then
drill a hole through the table
frame and the leg. (Try to
get someone to help you with
this.) A bolt with washer and
nut will hold the leg securely
in place.

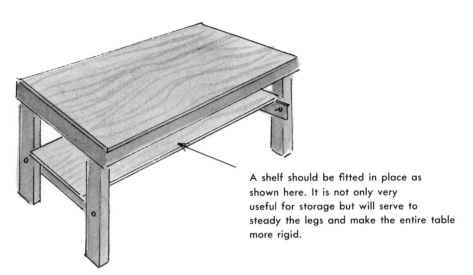

A shelf should be fitted in place as shown here. It is not only very useful for storage but will serve to steady the legs and make the entire table more rigid.

The work table can be made still more rigid by nailing a plank or piece of plywood onto the rear two legs. This will prevent any side-to-side swaying when vigorous sawing or planing is underway.

Glue, in addition to the nails, will make for a very rugged construction.

Make sure you have a good light.

A variety of smaller tools such as files, screwdrivers, wrenches, and so on, can be attached to a panel on the rear of the workbench.

If you are going to attach a woodworker's vise to your workbench, make provisions for fitting it in place before the entire project is completed. (A metal machinist's vise can be simply bolted onto a corner of the finished table.)

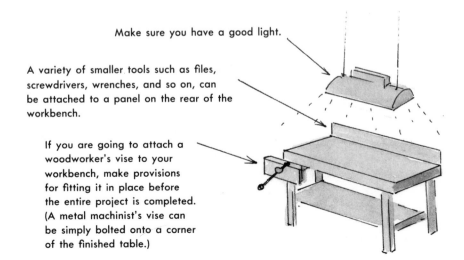

Ship Models

A stout block of wood and a few wood dowels are all that
are required to make a medium-sized ship model. The
model shown here is a display model—it is not intended
for the water. That means you don't have to worry about
sails or waterproof glues or careful balancing, or any of
the delicate little adjustments needed to get a model sail-
ing boat to perform properly.

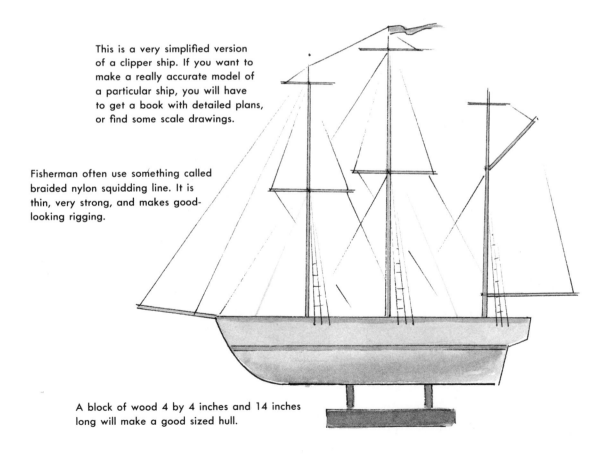

This is a very simplified version
of a clipper ship. If you want to
make a really accurate model of
a particular ship, you will have
to get a book with detailed plans,
or find some scale drawings.

Fisherman often use something called
braided nylon squidding line. It is
thin, very strong, and makes good-
looking rigging.

A block of wood 4 by 4 inches and 14 inches
long will make a good sized hull.

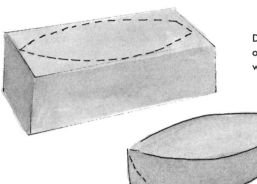

Draw the outline of the hull on the top of the block. Then cut away up to this line with a saw, chisel, or Surform tool.

After the looking-down-from-the-top shape has been cut out, draw the side profile. Then cut this out.

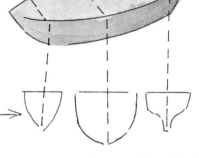

Round off the bottom edges. Try and get the smooth, flowing shapes that give a boat hull a sleek, graceful look.

A file and sandpaper will produce a smooth finish.

Cross-sectional "slices" of a clipper ship hull would look something like this. ——→

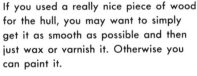

Thin wood dowels will make the spars. They should be tapered at the ends. The mast fits into holes drilled in the deck.

If you used a really nice piece of wood for the hull, you may want to simply get it as smooth as possible and then just wax or varnish it. Otherwise you can paint it.

Heavy, strong thread can be used for the rigging, and for attaching the spars. A drop of glue will keep knots from coming loose.

Two short pieces of dowel set into a board will make a stand. The dowels are then fitted into holes drilled in the bottom of the ship's hull.

A Dog House

A dog house is a rather ambitious undertaking, not because it is particularly difficult to build, but because usually it must be quite large (unless you have a miniature toy poodle, in which case it can be small!). It must be built so that it is weather tight, it must be strong, and it should look good. There is no point in simply throwing together a few pieces of plywood and calling them a dog house. The roof would probably leak, your dog wouldn't go near it, and you would have a bad feeling every time you looked at it.

Before you start to build you should have a conference with yourself—and with your dog! Decide what size your dog house should be. Do you have any materials on hand that you can use? Then sketch out some plans. They will give you an idea of what your dog house will look like and will tell you what materials you will be needing. The drawings on the next two pages suggest some possibilities and may give you some idea of how to proceed.

Two pieces of plywood
will make the roof.

The average dog house is basically
a simple box with peaked ends and
with an opening for the door.

When you plan the size, allow
room for your dog to move about
inside. He or she won't much like
being squeezed into a tight box.

Plywood ½ inch thick should be adequate
for even a large dog house. Be sure the
plywood is exterior grade. Thin paneling
intended for interior surfacing will not
hold up in the weather. Nails should be
galvanized.

You must cover the roof with roofing
paper, or shingles, or whatever
material you can lay your hands on
that will prevent rain from getting
inside. A snug, dry interior is
essential if your dog is going to
feel comfortable and at home.

The dog house must have a floor,
and you should spread a piece of
heavy plastic on the ground
under the floor. This will
keep out dampness.

Another way to keep out
dampness is to raise the
entire structure up off
the ground. A few flat
stones or bricks will
do the trick.

Whatever kind of roof you decide
to make, be sure there is an
overhang. This will keep rain
and snow off the walls.

Here's a chance to see what kind of architect you would be. Perhaps you have some ideas that will make a very special kind of doghouse . . . with a porch? a steeple? a skylight?

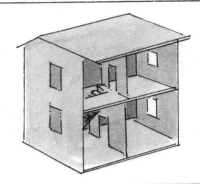

The sizes and proportions can be altered to make a dollhouse. Cut a few openings for windows and doors, add a staircase to the "second floor," make a partition or two, and you'll be ready to build furniture and decorate.

Toys

The illustrations here show a variety of simple toys that are easy to build yet make fine gifts for young children. They are very effective if sanded smooth and then varnished, though some people prefer to paint toys bright colors.

A great variety of toys can be made by simply combining various odd pieces of wood. For example, you could make a locomotive like this using an old broom or mop handle for the smokestack and steam dome. A discarded rolling pin would provide material for the boiler and wheels. A few other scraps of wood would make the cow catcher, cab, and so on.

Wheels can be made from slices cut off any round piece of wood. They can be attached by means of a long screw. You can drill a hole through the center of each wheel and then glue the wheels onto a dowel that will serve as an axle.

When cut-out animals are provided with wheels, they become pull-along toys, which young children are very fond of.

Additional details like ears cut from leather scraps, or tails made from braided ribbons, and a bright paint job will produce some very good looking toys.

If the mounting holes for the wheels are off center, the toy will waddle and lurch and bump along in a most interesting way.

A coping saw (see page 13) can cut curves and intricate shapes and is the ideal tool for making all sorts of realistic or imaginary animals and people.

Simple puppets, or figures with moving parts, can be made by cutting out separate parts from thin wood, then attaching them with wood screws.

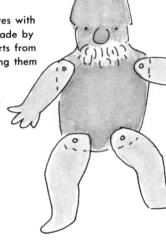

It isn't difficult to whittle all sorts of figures from a strip of 2 by 2 inch pine. The carving can be very simple, leaving the detailing to the paint and brush.

A platoon of good-looking soldiers can be used as bowling pins in a small-scale bowling game.

Many different kinds of balancing figures can be built like this. A length of stiff wire—like coat hanger wire—is attached to the figure by tape or thin nails. Then small, heavy lead weights are attached to the ends of the wire as shown. The center of gravity is now below the balancing point, and the figure will stand upright or, in this case, roll along a tight-rope wire.

-lead weight

The wheel must be free to turn and must have a groove around the edge.

Thin wood strips can be used to make all kinds of aircraft. Tongue depressors, popsicle sticks, and miscellaneous scraps can be put to use.

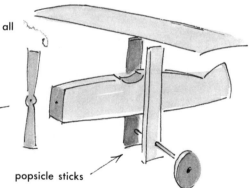

popsicle sticks

About the Author

Harvey Weiss has written and illustrated many popular books for children, among them *Model Buildings and How to Make Them, How to Run a Railroad: Everything You Need to Know About Model Trains, Model Airplanes and How to Build Them, How to Make Your Own Books, Model Cars and Trucks and How to Build Them, Ship Models and How to Build Them, Motors and Engines and How They Work,* and *How to Be an Inventor.* A distinguished sculptor whose work has received many awards and has been exhibited in galleries and museums across the country, he brings to his books a sure sense of what appeals to and can be accomplished by young people, and a sculptor's eye for simple, uncluttered forms.

"I've been working with wood for as long as I can remember," he writes. "I recall whittling little ship models from odd scraps of wood and making simple wood projects using dull tools in clumsy and incorrect ways—and only by luck and perseverance managing to get some kind of acceptable result. Thinking back on these beginning, uninformed adventures has prompted me to put this book together that explains some of the basic tools and methods of work that might otherwise seem quite mysterious."

Mr. Weiss is professor of sculpture at Adelphi University and lives in a much cluttered, old house in Greens Farms, Connecticut.